Netball

Bernie Blackall

Heinemann
LIBRARY

First published in Great Britain by Heinemann Library, Halley Court, Jordan Hill,
Oxford OX2 8EJ, a division of Reed Educational and Professional Publishing Ltd.
Heinemann is a registered trademark of Reed Educational & Professional Publishing Limited.

OXFORD MELBOURNE AUCKLAND
JOHANNESBURG BLANTYRE GABORONE
IBADAN PORTSMOUTH NH (USA) CHICAGO

Series cover and text design by Karen Young
Cover by Smarty-pants Design
Paged by Jo Pritchard
Edited by Jane Pearson
Illustrations by Joy Antonie
Picture research by Lara Artis
Production by Cindy Smith
Film separations by Typescan, Adelaide
Printed in Hong Kong by Wing King Tong

British Library Cataloguing in Publication Data
Blackall, Bernie
Netball. – (Top Sport)
1. Netball – Juvenile Literature
I . Title
796.3'24

ISBN 0 431 08514 5
This title is also available in hardback (ISBN 0 431 08510 2).

Acknowledgements
The Publishers would like to thank the following for permission to reproduce photographs:
Allsport/Stu Forster p 7. Australian Picture Library: (Allsport) p 9. Coo-ee Historical Picture Library:
p 8. Coo-ee Picture Library: p 5. Sportsframe/Robert Muir: p 20. Sue and Wies Fajzullin Photography:
cover, pp 4, 11, 12, 14, 15, 17, 18, 19, 21, 22, 23, 26, 27. Supersport/Eileen Langsley p 6.

Our thanks to Nuala Mullan for her assistance in the preparation of this book.

Every effort has been made to contact copyright holders of any material reproduced in this book.
Any omissions will be rectified in subsequent printings if notice is given to the Publisher.

Any words appearing in the text in bold, **like this**, are explained in the Glossary.

Contents

About netball

Netball is a non-contact sport played between two teams of seven players.

Each team aims to pass the ball into its **goal circle** so that the goal shooter and goal attack can score goals. In order to score, the ball must pass through the goal ring from above. Each team also aims to prevent the other team from scoring goals. The team with the most goals at the end of play is the winner.

Two umpires control the game from the sidelines. A game consists of 60 minutes of play, divided into four quarters of 15 minutes each, or 40 minutes of play divided into four quarters of 10 minutes each.

Beginning play

The two captains toss a coin for choice of goal end or first centre pass before the game begins. Play begins with one centre player beginning with a **centre pass**. The centre player will pass to a team-mate who must receive the ball within the **centre third** of the court.

The game is re-started after each goal is scored and at the beginning of each quarter in this manner, with teams taking possession alternately.

Whenever the ball passes out of court, it is brought back into play by the non-offending team with a throw-in from the sideline.

Each team aims to score goals by shooting the ball through the goal ring.

UK highlights

Netball is organised separately in England, Scotland, Wales and Northern Ireland, and each country has its own netball association. Players join a club and compete in local club and cup competitions. Good players are selected to play for their county, area or district, and the best players from these teams are chosen to play for their country – at under-17, under-19 or open age levels.

There are two main types of competitions. In league competitions every team plays each other throughout the season. In a cup competition only the winners of each game go through to the next round, until the final two teams meet. Again, competitions are organised by age group, so that everybody has a fair chance.

In England the winners of local leagues compete against each other in the national league.

Wales and England juniors competing in a FENA tournament

Good players are selected to play for their county or region, leading to the annual inter county or regional tournaments.

In Wales clubs can play in local league and cup competitions, and the best players are selected to play in the area league. These teams compete in the annual area championships.

Northern Ireland clubs compete in a league against teams from all over the country, culminating in the annual Shield competition. There are no area or county teams but good club players are selected to play for their country.

Scottish clubs compete in local leagues, the Scottish Clubs tournament and the Scottish Cup. Good club players are selected to play for their district in league and cup competitions.

International competition

The Federation of European Netball Associations (FENA) organises netball in Europe. The four countries of the United Kingdom compete every year in the FENA tournament.

The World Championships are held every four years. They took place in England in 1963 and 1995, and in Scotland in 1987. The nearest any UK team has come to winning was when England came second in 1975.

Commonwealth Games

Netball was included in the Commonwealth Games for the first time in Malaysia in 1998 and it was a great occasion. England won the bronze medal and Australia beat New Zealand in the final to win the gold medal. UK netball players are looking forward to the next Commonwealth Games in Manchester in 2002.

England playing Barbados at the 1998 Commonwealth Games

History of netball

Netball developed from the American game of basketball, which was invented by Dr James Naismith in Massachusetts in 1891. Visiting England in 1895, Dr Toll, an American, introduced basketball to the female students at Madame Osterberg's Physical Training College. The game was played on either a grass court or in a gymnasium with goals that consisted of clothes props for goal posts and waste paper baskets for baskets.

Women liked the game despite the fact that their long skirts, bustle backs, nipped waists and button-up shoes impeded running on the court and their 'leg of mutton' sleeves restricted arm movement and made dribbles and long passes difficult.

Basketball adapted

The women decided to adapt the game. They divided the court into thirds and introduced a rule that the ball must be caught or touched at least once in each third. No player was allowed to run with the ball, restricted playing areas were established for each position, and they increased the number of players to nine (later reduced to seven). They removed basketball backboards and allowed five seconds (later reduced to three) to shoot for goal. They modified the goal ring to suit a smaller ball.

A game of netball in Australia in 1930

Netball World Championships are held every four years.

The first rule book

In 1901 the Ling Association in England devised the Official Rules of netball and printed 250 rule books. These rules introduced a goal circle, the size of the ball and the goal ring were reduced and points were now scored instead of goals. As the game advanced baskets were used, but until someone realised it was best that they were open at the bottom – the umpires would have to use a ladder or shimmy up the pole to retrieve the ball after a goal was scored. Some game organisers were more advanced – they would use another pole to tilt the basket and remove the ball.

In the early 1900s, the game travelled to many British colonies and Commonwealth countries. New Zealand, Australia, United Kingdom, India, Malaysia, Africa and the West Indies still dominate international netball competitions.

International competition

International competition between Scotland, Wales and England began in 1949. Australia played New Zealand for the first time in 1938.

In 1960 the International Federation was formed. With all participating countries agreeing to an international code of rules, it was decided that an International Tournament would be held every four years.

What you need to play

The netball court is 30.5 metres long and 15.5 metres wide. It is divided into thirds:

- goal third (attack)
- centre third
- goal third (defence).

Play begins from the **centre circle** which is marked in the middle of the centre third. The semi-circles at either end of the court – the goal circles – are 4.9 metres in radius. Goals must be shot from inside these circles.

The goal post is 3.05 metres tall with a 38 centimetre diameter steel ring on top. An open net usually hangs from the ring. Junior players 10 years and under (playing modified rules) use a goal post that is 2.4 metres high.

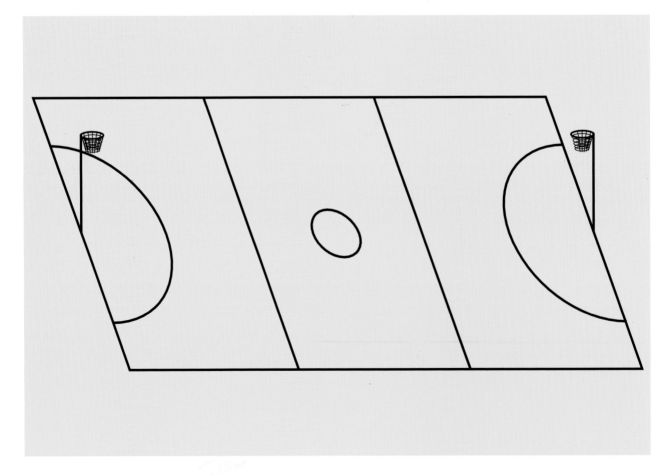

The ball

A netball is made from leather or rubber. Most matches are played with a size 5 ball which is 71 centimetres in circumference and weighs 450 grams. Junior players, 10 years and under, use a size 4 ball.

Clothing

Each of the seven players wears a coloured bib. The bib indicates in letters the position of the player on the court.

The centre player (C) links the play between the other players on the team – these are divided into **attackers** and **defenders**. The three attacking positions are:
• Goal Shooter (GS)
• Goal Attack (GA)
• Wing Attack (WA).

The three defending positions are:
• Goal Keeper (GK)
• Goal Defence (GD)
• Wing Defence (WD).

All players require strong defensive, as well as attacking, skills.

Girls usually wear a T-shirt and skirt. Boys play in shorts and T-shirt. Clothes and/or bibs are in team colours, making it easy to recognise team-mates and so that the umpires can easily distinguish between the teams.

Well-fitting sports shoes and cushioned socks will provide protection for your feet as you run, jump and land on the hard court surface.

Rules

There are four types of penalties in netball:

- free pass
- penalty pass or shot at goal
- toss up
- throw-in.

Free pass offences

When a minor **infringement** takes place a **free pass** is awarded to the non-offending team. It is taken from where the infringement occurred. A free pass is awarded when one of the following occurs.

Quickly assess your options as soon as you catch the ball.

Having landed on her right foot as she caught the ball, this player is permitted to step onto her left foot and lift her right foot. But she must pass the ball before she steps onto her right foot again.

Held ball

Once you have received the ball you must play it or shoot for goal within three seconds. When the ball comes to you, quickly assess your passing options and pass the ball or shoot for goal. If you hold it for three seconds or more, the umpire will signal 'held ball'. A player from the opposition will then take possession.

Footwork

Upon receiving the ball you are allowed to take just one step, either in the direction of the pass or to pivot and throw the ball. If you catch the ball with your weight on both feet, you may choose to step onto your left or your right foot. If you reground the foot that landed first while holding the ball or play it to yourself, a free pass is awarded to the opposing team.

Over a third

The ball must be touched in each third of the court as it travels from one end to the other. If the ball travels from a goal third across the centre third without being touched, the umpire will call 'over a third' and a free pass will be taken by the opposing team from the point where the ball entered the attacking third.

Offside

Each player is restricted in his or her playing areas. You are **offside** if you move out of your area whether you have possession of the ball or not.

Short pass

When the ball is passed, there must be enough space for a third player to move between the thrower and the receiver.

Shooting for goals

Each team's goal shooter and goal attack are the only players allowed to shoot for goal. They must be completely within the goal circle when they shoot.

Throw-in

When the ball goes outside the court area, play is re-started with a **throw-in**, which is taken by a member of the team who did not touch the ball last.

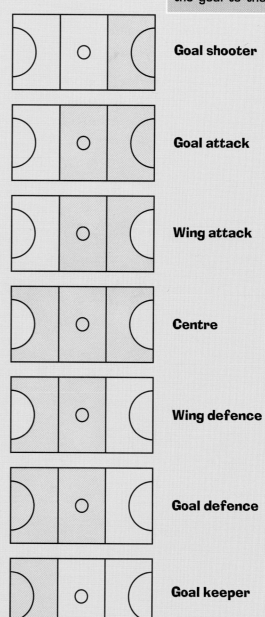

Goal shooter

Goal attack

Wing attack

Centre

Wing defence

Goal defence

Goal keeper

Rules

Penalties

Netball is a non-contact game. A **penalty pass** is awarded for infringements such as **obstruction** and **contact** which interferes with an opponent's play.

A penalty pass is awarded to the non-offending team. The offending player must stand to the side, completely out of play, until the ball is brought back into play.

The following infringements result in a penalty pass.

Contact

Contact which interferes with play is illegal. Even an accidental collision will result in a penalty pass or shot at goal being awarded.

When defending a player with the ball you must be at least 0.9 metres away.

Obstruction

When a team is defending, each player tries to limit its opponents' passes and shots for goal. A defender must remain at least 0.9 metres from the player with the ball. He or she can extend his or her arms to defend or intercept a pass, but may not touch the player with the ball.

A defending player may stand closer than 0.9 metres to a player who does not have the ball, but may not interfere with the throwing or shooting action.

You may not contact another player during a netball game, and you must be at least 0.9 metres away from a player with the ball.

Penalty pass or shot at goal

When a defender violates the contact or obstruction rule in the goal circle, a penalty pass or shot at goal is awarded. The defender must stand to the side while the shot at goal is taken. Once the ball has been released, the defender may then move back into play.

The toss up

When two opposing players infringe at the same time or grab the ball at the same time, the ball is put back into play with a **toss up**. Two opposing players stand 0.9 metres apart facing their goal end with their hands at their sides. The umpire holds the ball between them below shoulder height. The umpire then tosses the ball up no more than 60 centimetres, and blows a whistle to indicate that the players may move to try to catch it.

If two players offend at the same time, the ball is tossed up between them to resume play.

Skills

Playing a match

With regular practice you will become competent at all the skills of netball. Your coach will probably change your position on the court regularly so that you experience all aspects of the game and develop both attacking and defending skills.

Although all players need to master all the skills of the game, each player in the team has a particular role to play.

Each team member takes up position with their opponent at the start of play.

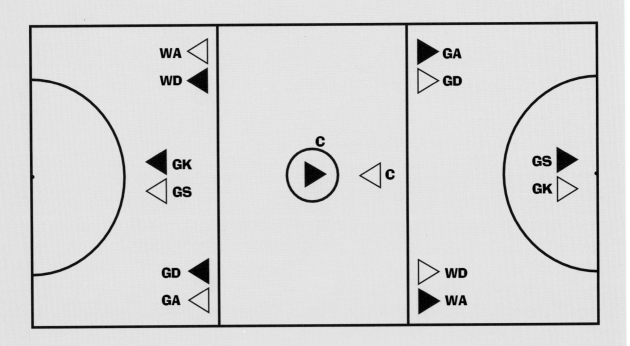

The goal shooter's main role is to shoot for goal.

Goal keeper

The goal keeper defends shots for goal made by the goal shooter of the opposing team. The goal keeper's role is also to prevent the ball from being passed.

Goal defence

The goal defence tries to prevent the opposing team's goal attack from getting the ball, and defends shots for goal.

Wing defence

The wing defence plays both an attacking and a defending role. He or she plays against the opposing team's wing attack and must prevent the wing attack from receiving the ball, and must break free to receive the ball to pass it towards the attacking third.

Centre

The centre plays in all areas of the court except the goal circles. This position requires rapid court movement and much stamina. He or she plays an attacking and a defending role depending on which team is in possession of the ball.

Wing attack

The wing attack works to give the goal attack and goal shooter opportunities to shoot for goal. He or she plays against the opposing team's wing defence. If the team lose possession of the ball, the wing attack must move into a defensive role against his or her opponent.

Goal attack

The goal attack should work with the goal shooter to provide the best option to shoot for goal. He or she must be a capable goal scorer. The goal attack must always be ready to grab a **rebound** for a second chance to shoot for goal.

Goal shooter

The goal shooter's main role is to shoot for goal, or to pass to the goal attack if he or she is better placed to score.

Skills

Footwork and balance

In a netball game you will run, change direction, jump and land at top speed, all within a small court area. Running with small steps, bent knees and with your weight on the balls of your feet will help you to react quickly to each situation.

It is only on rare occasions that you will receive the ball while you are stationary. When taking a catch on the run, your landing is important. Aim to land on one foot and then the other. The first foot is your pivoting foot. If you lift it, it must not be put back on the ground until you have passed the ball. Your second landing foot may be moved as many times as you like, as long as your pivoting foot remains on the ground. Move your stepping foot to change direction, or to help you balance.

To develop good **footwork**, practise running and landing on your right and then your left foot. Ask a team-mate to act as an opponent, and practise pivoting left and right to avoid him or her.

A well-balanced player has moved into position to pass the ball to a team-mate.

The chest pass is used when you want to pass the ball quickly and accurately over a short distance.

Passing the ball

It is important that you learn to pass the ball quickly and accurately towards a team-mate.

A good pass will avoid interception by an opponent and will be easy for the receiver to take. In many cases you will be passing to a receiver who is on the move. Always pass the ball ahead of the receiver to the space into which your team-mate will run. Your receiver should catch the ball with outstretched hands.

For all passes, use your fingers and wrists to power the ball accurately to the target. A fast accurate pass will be harder for your opponents to intercept. You should always step in the direction which your pass will travel – this will add speed and power to your pass.

There are a number of passes which you will use in a game. These are:
• the chest pass
• the shoulder pass
• the bounce pass
• the lob pass
• the overhead pass.

The chest pass

The chest pass is a fast and powerful two-handed pass made over a short distance. The ball should travel horizontally, straight to your team-mate's chest.

With your hands spread behind the ball, flick the ball forward as you step towards your target.

Skills

The shoulder pass

The shoulder pass is the most common pass used in netball. It is a one-handed pass used to throw the ball over long distances.

With your arm extended and your fingers spread behind the ball, hold it at shoulder height. Standing side on, step toward your target. Bring your hand over your shoulder and use your fingers as you thrust your arm forward to release the ball.

A good bounce pass should remain low, reaching your team-mate below waist-height.

Practise this skill with both your left and your right arm so that you are able to confuse your opponents or pass the ball quickly if you receive it with your non-throwing hand.

The shoulder pass is used to pass the ball over a long distance.

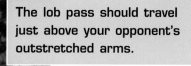

The lob pass should travel just above your opponent's outstretched arms.

The lob pass

When you throw a lob pass, the ball travels in a high arc, over an opponent's head, and into a team-mate's hands. Throw the lob with one hand. It is often used to pass the ball to the goal shooter or goal attack in the goal circle, avoiding a defender.

The overhead pass

This pass is often used when you have caught a pass or a rebound high above your head. It is an effective means of passing the ball quickly to a team-mate.

The bounce pass

This pass is ideal when you are finding it difficult to avoid an opponent. It is often used in a crowded goal circle to get the ball through to a team-mate in a good position to shoot for goal. The bounce pass can be thrown from one or both hands.

With your fingers spread behind the ball, bend low and push the ball strongly from about hip height. The ball should bounce about two thirds of the way to the receiver, coming up to be caught at between knee- and waist-height.

Push the ball forwards with both hands from behind your head for the overhead pass.

Skills

Shooting goals

It is up to the goal shooter and the goal attack to finish the good work of the rest of the team. No matter how good the team is – if these two players cannot get the ball through the ring, then all efforts are wasted.

In order to be a good shooter you will need lots of practice to build your aim, confidence, and concentration. Frequent practice from all parts of the goal circle is essential. The following steps will help you shoot accurately for the goal:

• Stand facing the goal post, feet parallel and shoulder-width apart.

• Hold the ball with the fingers of one hand above your head. Put your other hand on the side of the ball for balance.

• Let your wrists drop back slightly behind your head, and bend your knees.

• Push the body weight up, releasing the ball from above your head with a flick of the wrist.

• The ball should travel in a high arc and descend through the ring.

Bend your knees to give you spring as you release the ball.

Rebounding

Whenever a shot misses and rebounds from the goal, an opportunity exists for both shooters and defenders to grab the ball.

To receive a rebound well, try to anticipate the flight of the ball and judge where it will rebound to. Try to position yourself so that your opponent is blocked out. Jump as the ball bounces off the ring to be the first to grab it.

Catching the ball

You need to take great care when you are receiving the ball. Catching is an essential skill – you must be able to catch with a safe pair of hands so that you can then pass the ball before your opponent has a chance to block your pass.

Provide a good target for the passer by moving into a space clear of opponents. As you receive the ball grasp it strongly with outstretched hands. Keep your thumbs behind the ball to prevent it slipping through.

Grasp the ball with outstretched hands.

Skills

Attacking skills

Every player in your team is in attack from the moment a team member gains possession of the ball. Your aim in attack is to get the ball safely and quickly to your goalers who will then try to score.

An effective attack demands accurate passing and catching. But your movement on the court – **leading**, finding space, turning behind a defender and protecting space – are all critical for an effective attack.

At times a close-checking opponent will make it difficult to move into a clear position to receive a pass.

Move quickly to the left or right. Your opponent will follow as he or she wants to prevent you breaking clear.

Now move behind your opponent into the open space to receive the ball.

Leading

Leading is running straight towards the ball, beating your opponent with speed to take possession.

Dodging behind a defender

If your opponent is checking you closely, you can dodge behind him or her to break free. Run out fast, or lead, to one side, then quickly double back behind your opponent to break free and receive the pass. Such a sudden change of direction is usually successful in confusing or wrong-footing a close checking defender.

Protecting space

Your body can be legally used as a barrier to stop your opponent from moving into the area where you want to catch the ball. Keep yourself edged in front of your opponent, taking care not to contact him or her. Then, as the ball is thrown, move forward quickly to catch it.

Stand with your back to your opponent.

Lunge quickly to catch the ball in the space you have protected.

Skills

Defending skills

When your opponents have possession of the ball, your team has two aims:
• to regain possession
• to prevent your opponents from scoring.

Good defending skills will increase your chances of winning back the ball or preventing a goal. Every team member must try to get the ball back by forcing the other side to make mistakes by limiting their space and by intercepting passes.

A defensive stance

A good defensive stance requires you to stand with feet shoulder-width apart. With knees slightly bent and arms relaxed by your side you are ready to react and/or intercept. If your opponent has the ball, you can defend from in front. You must not be closer than 0.9 metres, but you can extend your arms to try to intercept the pass.

Be ready to throw your arms in the air to intercept a high pass or to force your opponent into a less accurate shot.

Defending

'**Man to man**' is a very common method of defending. It involves keeping your body slightly in front of your opponent to try to keep him or her out of the action.

Defending the shot for goal

The goal keeper and the goal defence are the two players who may defend the opposing team's goal shooter and goal attack, to prevent them scoring. They must try to prevent the goal shooter and goal attack from receiving the ball in the goal circle. If an attacking player is about to shoot for goal, the defender must stand 0.9 metres away, but can lean forward with an arm outstretched to try to intercept the ball or to break the concentration of the shooter.

Players defending in the goal circle should always be ready to catch a rebound and to pass the ball quickly towards their own goal.

Getting ready

To avoid injury and perform at your best, warm-up with these activities before training or playing. Loose and supple muscles are much less likely to be strained. Start by running around the court twice in each direction.

Side bends
Stand upright with one hand on your waist. Bring your other hand up over your head as you bend to the side. Make sure you don't lean forward as you bend.

Star jumps
Stand with your feet together and your arms by your sides. Jump up and land with your feet apart and your arms outstretched. Then jump back to the start position. Repeat 10–15 times.

Treadmills
Put your hands on the ground, shoulder-width apart, and stretch your legs out behind you. Bring one foot forward. Replace it and then bring the other foot up. Repeat 10–15 times.

Shoulder stretch
Stretch one arm
across your body.
Use your other hand
to pull your elbow
into your chest until
you feel the stretch.

Calf stretch
Stand with one foot about
one metre in front of the
other. Bend your leading
leg and lean forward,
keeping both feet
flat on the floor.

Arm circles
Stretch your arms
above your head and
then take them around
in circles, forwards
and then backwards,
stretching as far up
and around as you can.

Lower back stretch
Lie on your back with your legs
outstretched. Bend one knee up
to your chest and lift your head
and shoulders off the floor to
meet it. Lower yourself slowly
back to the floor and then
repeat with the other leg.

Taking it further

England

All England Netball Association
Netball House
9 Paynes Park
Hitchin
Hertfordshire SG5 1EH
Tel: 01462 442344

English Sports Council
16 Upper Woburn Place
London WC1 0QP
Tel: 0171 273 1500

Northern Ireland

Northern Ireland Netball Association
Netball Office
House of Sport
2A Upper Malone Road
Belfast BT9 5LA
Tel: 01232 381222

Northern Ireland Sports Council
House of Sport
2A Upper Malone Road
Belfast BT9 5LA
Tel: 01232 381222

Scotland

Scottish Netball Association
24 Ainslie Road
Hillington Business Park
Hillington
Glasgow G52 4RU
Tel: 0141 570 4016

Scottish Sports Council
Caledonia House
South Gyle
Edinburgh EH12 9DQ
Tel: 0131 317 7200

Wales

Welsh Netball Association
50 Cathedral Road
Cardiff CF1 9LL
Tel: 01222 237048

Sports Council for Wales
Sophia Gardens
Cardiff CF1 9SW
Tel: 01222 300500

Further reading

Know the Game: Netball, AENA/A & C Black Publishers, London, 1998
Mullan, N. *Successful Sports: Netball*, Heinemann Library, Oxford, 1996
Galsworthy, B. *Netball*, Crowood Press, Wiltshire, 1996
Lloyd, G., Jeffris, D. *Sports Skills: Netball*, Wayland Publishers, East Sussex, 1993
Shakespear, W. *Netball: Steps to Success*, Human Kinetics, Champaign, IL, 1997

Glossary

attackers players on the team that has possession of the ball

contact an illegal interference where a player pushes, bumps or holds an opponent

centre circle the small circle in the centre of the court from which play is started, or restarted after a goal

centre third middle third of the court

centre pass the pass from the centre circle, used to start play and to restart after a goal

defenders players on the team that does not have possession of the ball. Defenders use many tactics to prevent their opponents from attacking.

footwork the rule regarding the movement of a player's feet when in possession of the ball

free pass a pass awarded to the non-offending team for an infringement. Any player allowed in this area of the court is allowed to take the pass.

goal circle the semi-circle which marks the area from which players may shoot for goal

infringement when a player violates a netball rule

leading running into a space to receive the ball

man to man standing close to your opponent to restrict his or her opportunities to receive the ball

obstruction when an opposing team member defends while closer than 0.9 metres to a player in possession of ball

offside an infringement caused when any player moves into a playing area other than their own. A free pass is awarded to the opposition team.

penalty pass pass awarded to the non-offending team when an infringement occurs against them. If the infringement occurs in the goal circle, a penalty pass or shot at goal is awarded.

rebound players from both teams compete for the ball as it bounces off the goal post into play from a missed shot at goal

throw-in the means of returning the ball back into play when it has gone out of court

toss up the umpire throws the ball up between two opposing players who have caught a ball, or infringed, at the same time

Index